I0161622

Printed in the USA

Mayanmar Language:

101 Burmese Verbs

BY NAKAJI NAY WIN

Contents

Introduction to Burmese Verbs

Meaning of a Verb

Basically, there are 8 parts of speech in Burmese Grammar, which we called "War Sin Ga," and the Verb ("Tre Yar" in Burmese) is one of them. Verbs are action words that can indicate having, being, acting or doing. Most Burmese sentences are dominated by the verb and its suffixes.

Burmese verb roots are almost always suffixed with at least one particle, which conveys such information as tense, intention, politeness, mood, etc. This rooted verb neither changes nor agrees with the subject in person, number, or gender. (Ref: Wikipedia)

For example: We can root action verb called "စား" [Sa'], which alone means "eat," and it is very imperative because when we suffix with the word that represents present tense, "တယ်" [tal] (literally "သည်" [de]), it becomes present action and/or a factual statement; "စားသည်," which means "I eat".

Similarly, when we combine that root verb with past tense suffix "ခဲ့သည်" [Ke' di], the statement becomes past action, "စားခဲ့သည်" [Sa' Ke' de]. Now, you can see that the root verb can be suffixed with corresponding tense words, perform statements, and command words to show different statements and times of eating.

You will learn more about Burmese Verbs in following examples and statements, which are quite fun and interesting.

Original or root verbs are used to express an action (I eat), a state of being (I am), or a state of having (he has). The present tense in Burmese conveys a situation or event in the present time. If you want to say or write in present tense, simply suffix "De" behind the root verb.

Here are some examples of verbs according to their types of meanings.

Three types of meanings   Example

1. Acting   write, read, eat, speak
2. Being   be, fall, break
3. Having   has, locate,

When you want to use these action verbs for present time, suffix "သည်" [de] (you can pronounce: 'the') behind the verb and it becomes present action tense. In order to complete the sentence, we can put a subject in front of the verb. Remember, "tal" is similar in meaning to "[de]," which is used in verbal statements. On the other hand, [de] is more literally used in writing statements.

Meaning	Verbs	Suffix (Present tense)	Result
Acting	write ရေး (Yae)	[De]/tal သည်/ တယ်	He writes သူရေးသည်။ (တယ်။) Thu yae de / (tal)
Being	red နီ (Ni)	[De]/tal သည်/ တယ်	It is red နီသည်/တယ် Ni de /tal
Having	have ရှိ (Shi)	[De]/tal သည်/ တယ်	I have ရှိ သည်/တယ် Shi de/tal

If you want to say or write about past time, you might need to suffix "ခဲ့သည်" [Ke' De] behind that original verb, or root verb. You will see more of these as you learn.

Meaning	Verbs	Suffix (Past tense)	Result
Acting	Read ဖတ် (Phat)	Ke' [De]/tal ခဲ့သည်/ တယ်	Read ဖတ်ခဲ့သည်။ (တယ်) Phat Ke' de / (tal)
Being	Break ကွဲ (Kwal)	Ke' [De]/tal ခဲ့သည်/ တယ်	Broke ကွဲခဲ့သည်/တယ် Kwal Ke' de /tal
Having	Have ရှိ (Shi)	Ke' [De]/tal ခဲ့သည်/ တယ်	Had ရှိ ခဲ့သည်/တယ် Shi Ke' de/tal

If you want to say or write in the future tense, you can suffix "Mae" or "laint Mae" behind the root verb. For written statements, you can suffix the phrase "La Tan" behind the verb. The future tense in Burmese conveys a situation or event that is anticipated to happen in the future. Here are some examples:

Meaning	Verbs	Suffix (Future tense)	Result
Acting	Go သွား (Twar)	Mae မယ်	I will go ငါ သွားမယ်။ Nga Twar Mae
Being	Fall ချော်လဲ (Chal Lal)	Mae မယ်	You will fall ချော်လဲ မယ်။ Chal Lal Mae
Having	Have ရှိ (Shi)	Mae မယ်	I will have ရှိ လိမ့် မယ် Shi laint Mae

Important Note: The verb is one of the 8 Burmese parts of speech. Verbs in Burmese indicate having, being, acting, or doing. Burmese verbs roots are almost always suffixed with at least one particle, which conveys such information as tense, intention, politeness, mood, etc.

If you want to speak or write in the present tense, suffix "De" or "Tal". For past tense, suffix "Ke' De," and for future tense, suffix "Mae" or "laint Mae" in vebal conversations, and "လတ္တံ့" (La tan) in writing. You can learn more in the coming chapter, "Tenses."

Now we will continue to three types of components in Burmese Verbs as follows;

Three type of components	Example
1. Original verb	write, read, eat, speak
2. Adjective	pretty, sweet, pleasant
3. Compound (adverb)	having meal, painting, quicken

So far, we learned that original verbs or root verbs are used with suffixes that show present, past, or future tenses. We might also need to learn some original/root verbs and their meanings. Here are some original verbs with their Burmese pronunciations and English meanings.

Original/ Root Verbs	Burmese Pronunciation	English Meaning
ဝင်	Win	Go in
ထွက်	Htwet	Go out
သွား	Twar	Go
လာ	Lar	Come
စား	Sar	Eat
သောက်	Tout	Drink
ပျောက်	Pyout	Lost
ကွဲ	Kwal	Break
အိပ်	Eight	Sleep
ကူညီ	Ku Nyi	Help
ရှိ	Shi	Have

ဖတ်	Phat	Read
ရေး	Yay	Write
ပြော	Pyaw	Speak
ချော်လဲ	Chal lal	Fall

These verbs can be used with a subject in front of them, and are followed by a suffix. The sentence looks like this: Subject + Verb + Suffix.

Here are some examples:

Subject + Verb + Suffix	Burmese writing
I + eat + suffix	ငါ+စား+တယ် Nga + Sar + De
He + read + suffix	သူ+ဖတ်+တယ် Thu + Phat + De
They + write + suffix	သူတို့ +ရေး+တယ် Thu Doe + Yay + De
We + speak + suffix	ငါတို့+ ပြော+တယ် Nga Doe + Pyaw + De

The suffix must follow the verb at all times. Depending on the situation, different suffixes can be used, such as ပြီ (Pyi), သည် (De), နှဲ (Nae), တော့ (Dot), မယ် (Mae), or ဘူး (Bu). "Pyi" is an agreement suffix, "Nae" and "Dot" are command suffixes, and "Bu" is used in negative statements.

Negative sentence

If you want to spreak or write sentences in the negative, the original/root verb must be surrounded by "Ma" in front of it, and "Nae" behind it.

Thus, the negative sentence is formed with **Ma + Verb + Nae,** which means "Don't."

Here are some examples:

	Don't eat မ+စား+နဲ့ Ma sar +nae	Suffix Ma + Verb + Nae (Don't)
	Don't come မလာ+ နဲ့ Ma lar +nae	Ma + Verb + Nae (Don't)
Comparative	Don't do it မလုပ်+နဲ့ Ma lote +nae	Ma + Verb + Nae (Don't)
	Don't go there မသွား+နဲ့ Ma twar+ nae	Ma + Verb + Nae (Don't)

In response to a command or order in a negative sentence, we put the same sequence, but have to change the suffix behind the verb to the word "Bu." So, the sentence looks like **Ma+Verb+Bu**, which means "won't." You can see some examples in the following table.

	I won't eat မစား+ဘူး Ma sar +bu	Suffix Ma + Verb + Bu (Won't)
	I won't come မလာ+ ဘူး Ma lar +bu	Ma + Verb + Bu (Won't)

	I won't do it မလုပ်+ ဘူး Ma lote +bu	Ma + Verb + Bu (Won't)
Negative response	I won't go there မသွား+ ဘူး Ma twar+ bu	Ma + Verb + Bu (Won't)

Type 2 — Adjectives: Sometimes, when we suffix "သည်" [De] behind the adjective, it creates a modified verb that shows the quality of the specific noun. In Burmese, we call it "ဂုဏ်ရည်ပြ ကြိယာ" [Gone Yee Pya Tri Yar].

For example, beautiful "လှ" ("Hla") is an adjective, and when it is followed by the suffix "De," it becomes the verb that shows the quality of beauty: "Hla De," which means "you are beautiful." Here are some more examples:

Adjective	Suffix	Verb
Beautiful - လှ (hla)	သည် (de)	လှသည် (Hla De)
Sweet - ချို (cho)	သည် (de)	ချို သည် (Cho De)
Popular - ထင်ရှား(Htin shar)	သည် (de)	ထင်ရှားသည် (Htin Shar De)

Type 3 of Compound Verbs

In Burmese grammar, verbs can be compounded to become more specific and effective ways to express an action or state of being. Two or more original verbs can be combined together to become one specific compound verb. In Burmese, we call compound verbs "Paung Sat Tri Yar."

V+V	Suffix	Final Verb
Eat +drink - စား+ သောက်(Sar+ taunt)	သည် (de)	စားသောက်သည် Sar Taunt De
Darw+ paint - ရေးခြယ် (yae+ chae)	သည် (de)	ရေးခြယ် သည် Yae Chae De

Sometimes, you can combine more than two original/root verbs to form one compound verb. This combination is used to specify continuous actions and can express the sequence of actions. For example:

Verb + verb	Composing	Compound Verb + Suffix	Meaning
Come + go	ဝင်ထွက်+ သွားလာ Win htwet + Twar Lar	ဝင်ထွက် သွားလာသည်	Comes and goes
Arrive+ award + support	ကြရောက်+ ချီးမြှင့်+ အားပေး Kya yout + Chee Myint + Arr pay	ကြရောက် ချီးမြှင့် အားပေး သည်	Acclaim

8

Tense

Like English grammar, Burmese also has tenses. Depending on the time and situation, the tense changes. When you describe a tense, the root/original verb doesn't change, but the suffix word does. To be noted: Burmese verbs do not have to agree with the number, gender or person of their subjects. Neither singular nor plural verb forms are stressed.

In a simple tense, Burmese verbs do not necessarily have to use a subject. For example: I eat; . she goes; we sleep. In these three sentences, the subjects "I," "she," and "we" can be left alone when you speak in Burmese. However, the suffix must be added in order to form the correct tense.

For example:

In English, the phrase would be formed like "I+eat," but in Burmese, we say "eat+ suffix" (Sar + De/tal).

Voice	Tense	E.g	Burmese	Suffix
Active	Simple tense	I eat She eats We eat	စား Sar	စား+တယ် Sar tal
Passive	Simple tense	He was beaten	ရိုက်ခံရ Yai kan Ya	ရိုက်ခံရ+တယ် Yai kan Ya + tal

In spoken language, the simple present, past and future tenses are very similar. The original root of the verb (go- သွား) does not change in all tenses. Only the suffix will be changed in most of the paragraphs.

		Tense		
		Present (De/ Tal)	Past (Ke' De)	Future (Mae)
Aspect	Simple	သွားတယ် (go) Twar De	သွားခဲ့တယ် (went) Twar Ke' De	သွားမယ် (will go) Twar Mae
	Continuous	သွားတော့မယ် (going to go) Twar Dot Mae	သွားနေခဲ့တယ် (was going)	သွားလိမ့်မယ် (will be going)

			Twar Nay Ke' Tal [De]	Twar Late Mae
Perfect	သွားပြီ (has gone) Twar Pyi		သွားခဲ့ပြီး (had gone) Twar Ke' Pyeee	သွားပြီးလိမ့်မယ် (will have gone) Twar Pyee Late Mae
Perfect Continuous	သွားနေပြီ (has been going) Twar Nay Pyi		သွားပြီးသွားပြီ (had been going) Twar Pyee Twar Pyi	သွားပြီးသွားလိမ့်မယ် (will have been going)

In the table above, you can see a lot of suffixes after the verb. Original verbs alone cannot complete the sentence, but with the specific suffix, verbs can change into specific tenses.

The present Continuous tense is used for current situations. For continuous tense, we put "နေ" (Nay) between the root verb and the suffix word.

For example:

What are you doing? ဘာလုပ်နေတာလဲ - (Bar lote nae lae?)

I am reading. စာဖတ်နေတယ် -(szar phat nay tal [De])

Where are you going? ဘယ်သွားမလို့လဲ- (Bae twar ma loe lae?)

Going to a movie. ရုပ်ရှင်သွားကြည့်မလို့ (Yote shin twar kyi ma loe)

Please note that the suffixes in these two sentences are different. The question sentences start with "Bar," which means "What," and "Bae," which means "Where." Behind the root verb (are), the question suffix "lae" follows. For the first answer, as it is continuous, we must attach the suffix "Nay tal [De]" to the original verb "phat."

In second example, "twar" (go) and "kyi" (see) are original verbs, and "twar kyi" is a compound verb, which means "go and see."

Conjugation

The verb is a pretty complicated part of speech in Burmese grammar. In Burmese text, verbs meaning was have, state, and act. However, in the conversation, verbs are sometimes not clearly conjugated. Depending upon the situation, verbs can become adverbs or adjectives.

For example, verbs and adjectives in Burmese sentences are not visibly conjugated: "she is beautiful" (*beautiful* used as an adverb), and "beautiful girl" (*beautiful* used as an adjective) in English, but in Burmese, "beautiful" ("Hla") is used as root verb together with a suffix and a subject to mention that she is beautiful ("Thu Hla De").

Another example: "You are a bad boy" (*bad* used as an adverb), and "bad boy" (*bad* used as an adjective) in English; "bad" ("Soe") is used as a root verb in Burmese.

Similar to English, verbs can also be used as adverbs, adjectives, or nouns.

For example, present participles — cooking, reading, eating — can be used as a noun form, an adjective form, or an adverb form.

In the noun form of the present participle — the suffix will be မှု (muu) or ခြင်း (chin).

For example, "cooking" will be "ချက်ပြုတ်ခြင်း (chat pyat chin)" or "ချက်ပြုတ်မှု (chat Pyat muu)."

In the adjective form of the present participle — the suffix will be သော (thaw) or သည့် (dee).

For example: "reading" will be "စာဖတ်သော (szar phat thaw)" or "စာဖတ်သည့် (szar phat dee)."

In the adverb form of the present participle — the suffix will be "သောကြောင့် (thaw kyaunt - the reason form of the adverb)" or "လျှက် (leaat - manger form of the adverb)."

For example: "စာဖတ်များသော ကြောင့် (szar phat myar thaw kyaunt)" or "စာဖတ်လျှက် (szar phat leaat)."

The past participles of verbs can also be seen as adverbs and adjectives in Burmese language.

Similar to present participles, the suffix will be "သော (thaw)" for adjectives and "လျှက် (leaat)" for adverbs.

Tone mark	none or ——	ǀ	＼	／
Tone	Flat	High	Falling	Raising

Verb (Accept)	Conjugate	Translation	Transliteration	Affix
Present Tense	I accept the terms	ငါစည်းမျဉ်းများလက်ခံသည်	Ngr See Myin Myar Lat ken de	de
Past Tense	He accepted the terms	သူစည်းမျဉ်းများလက်ခဲ့သည်	Thu See Myin Myar Lat ken **ke de**	Ke
Future Tense	I will accept the terms	ငါစည်းမျဉ်းများလက်ခံလတ္တံ့	Ngr See Myin MyarLat ken la tan	La tan
Continuous	They are accepting the terms	သူတို့စည်းမျဉ်းများလက်ခံဆဲ	Thu toe See Myin MyarLat ken se	se

Verb (Admit)	Conjugate	Translation	Transliteration	Affix
Present Tense	I admit	ငါဝန်ခံသည်	Ngr Wan ken de	de
Past Tense	He admitted	သူဝန်ခံခဲ့သည်	Thu wan ken ke de	Ke
Future Tense	They will admit	သူတို့ဝန်ခံလတ္တံ့	Thu tot wan ken la tan	La tan
Continuous	She is admitting	သူဝန်မခံဆဲ	Thu ma wan ken se	se

Verb (Answer)	Conjugate	Translation	Transliteration	Affix
Present Tense	I answer the questions	ငါမေးခွန်းကိုတုံ့ပြန်သည်	Ngr may khun ko tone pyan de	de
Past Tense	They answered the phone	သူတို့ဖုန်းဖြင့်တုံ့ပြန်ခဲ့သည်	Thu tot phone phyinttone pyan ke de	Ke
Future Tense	She will answer your phone	သူမမင်းဖုန်းကိုတုံ့ပြန်လတ္တံ့	Thu ma min phone ko tone pyan la tan	La tan
Continuous	He is answering your phone	သူမမင်းဖုန်းကိုတုံ့ပြန်ဆဲ	Thu Min phone ko tone pyan se	Se

Verb (Appear)	Conjugate	Translation	Transliteration	Affix
Present Tense	I appear at your house	ငါမင်းအိမ်မှာပေါ်လာသည်	Ngr Min Eain mhr Paw lar de	De
Past Tense	They appeared at school	သူတို့ကျောင်းမှာပေါ်လာခဲ့သည်	Thu tot Kyaung mhr Paw lar ke de	Ke
Future Tense	She Will appear at school	သူမကျောင်းမှာပေါ်လာလတ္တံ့	Thu ma kyaung mhr Paw lar la tan	La tan
Continuous	He is appearing	သူပေါ်လာဆဲ	Thu Paw lar se	se

14

MAYANMAR LANGUAGE: 101 BURMESE VERBS

Verb (Ask)	Conjugate	Translation	Transliteration	Affix
Present Tense	I ask you	ငါမင်းကိုမေးမြန်းသည်	Ngar min ko Mae myan de	de
Past Tense	They asked me	သူတို့ငါ့ကိုမေးမြန်းခဲ့သည်	Thu tot nga ko Mae myan ke de	Ke
Future Tense	He will ask his way	သူသူ့နည်းလမ်းအတိုင်းမေးမြန်းလတ္တံ့	Thu thu nee lan atine ၊ Mae myan la tan	La tan
Continuous	She is asking her way	သူမနည်းလမ်းအတိုင်းမေးမြန်းဆဲ	Thu thu ma nee lan atine Mae myan se	se

Verb (To be)	Conjugate	Translation	Transliteration	Affix
Present Tense	I am a teacher	ငါဆရာဖြစ်သည်	Ngr saya Phit de	de
Past Tense	They were students	သူတို့ကျောင်းသားဖြစ်ခဲ့သည်	Thu tot kyaung thr Phit ke de	Ke
Future Tense	It will be a good movie	ရုပ်ရှင်ကောင်းဖြစ်လတ္တံ့	yote shin kaung Phit la ၊ tan	La tan
Continuous	It is raining	မိုးရွာနေဆဲ	Moe ywa nay se	se

Verb (To be able to)	Conjugate	Translation	Transliteration	Affix
Present Tense	I am able to read	ငါဖတ်နိုင်သည်	/ Ngar phat nai de	de
Past Tense	They were able to travel	သူတို့ခရီးသွားနိုင်ခဲ့သည်	Thu tot kha yee thwr / nai ke de	Ke
Future Tense	She will be able to read	သူမဖတ်နိုင်လိမ့်မည်	/ ၊ thu ma phat nai lame mi	Lame mi
Continuous				

Verb (Become)	Conjugate	Translation	Transliteration	Affix
Present Tense	I become a teacher	ငါဆရာဖြစ်လာသည်	Ngr saya Phit lar de	de
Past Tense	They became cooks	သူတို့စားဖိုမှူးဖြစ်လာခဲ့သည်	Thu tot sa pho mhu Phit lar ke de	Ke
Future Tense	He will become a star	သူနာမည်ကြီးဖြစ်လာလိမ့်မည်	Thu nan mae kyeePhit lar lame mi	Lame mi
Continuous	It is becoming difficult.	ပိုပိုခက်ခဲလာဆဲ	Po po khat ke lar se	se

Verb (Begin)	Conjugate	Translation	Transliteration	Affix
Present Tense	I begin to cry.	ငါစငိုမိသည်	Ngr Sa ngo mi de	de
Past Tense	They began to cry	သူတို့စငိုခဲ့မိသည်	Thu tot Sa Ngo ke mi de	Ke
Future Tense	He will begin to cry	သူတို့စငိုလိမ့်မည်	Thu tot Sa Ngo lame mi	Lame mi
Continuous	She is beginning crying	သူမစငိုနေဆဲ	Thu ma Sa ngo nay se	se

Verb (Break)	Conjugate	Translation	Transliteration	Affix
Present Tense	I break the cup	ငါခွက်ကိုခွဲသည်	Ngr kwat ko khwe de	de
Past Tense	They broke the glass	သူတို့ဖန်ခွက်ကိုခွဲခဲ့သည်	Thu tot kwat ko khwe ke de	Ke
Future Tense	He will break something	သူတစ်ခုခုကိုခွဲလိမ့်မည်	Thu ta khu khu ko khwe lame mi	Lame mi
Continuous	It is breaking	အဲဒါကျိုးတော့မည်	e dr Kyoe tot mi	se

Verb (Breathe)	Conjugate	Translation	Transliteration	Affix
Present Tense	I breathe the fresh air	ငါလေကောင်းလေသန့်ကိုရှုရှိက်သည်	Ngr lay kaung lay thant ko shu shite de	de
Past Tense	They breathed polluted air	သူတို့ညစ်ညမ်းတဲ့လေကိုရှုရှိက်ခဲ့သည်	Thu tot nyit nyan te lay ko she shite ke de	Ke
Future Tense	He will breathe clear air	သူလေသန့်ကိုရှုရှိက်လိမ့်မည်	Thu lay thant ko shu shite lame mi	Lame mi
Continuous	She is breathing nice air	သူမကောင်းသောလေကို ရှုရှိက်နေဆဲ	Thu ma kaung thaw lay ko shu shite nay se	se

Verb (Buy)	Conjugate	Translation	Transliteration	Affix
Present Tense	I buy a book	ငါစာအုပ်ဝယ်သည်	Ngr sar ote Wei de	de
Past Tense	They bought a computer	သူတို့ကွန်ပြူတာဝယ်ခဲ့သည်	Thu tot computer Wei ke de	Ke
Future Tense	He will buy an iPhone	သူအိုင်ဖုန်းဝယ်လိမ့်မည်	Thu iPhone Wei lame mi	Lame mi
Continuous	She is buying coffee	သူမကော်ဖီဝယ်နေဆဲ	Thu ma coffee Wei nay se	se

17

Verb (To call)	Conjugate	Translation	Transliteration	Affix
Present Tense	I call my mother	ငါ့ဲ့အမေကိုဖုန်းခေါ် ဆိုသည်	Ngr nga amay ko phone Kall so de	de
Past Tense	They called you	သူတို့မင်းကိုဖုန်းခေါ် ဆိုခဲ့သည်	Thu tot min ko phone Kall so ke de	Ke
Future Tense	He will call 911	သူ၉၁၁ကိုခေါ် ဆိုလိမ့်မည်	Thu 911 ko Kall so lame mi	Lame mi
Continuous	She is calling for help	သူမမင်းကိုခေါ် ဆိုနေဆဲ	Thu ma min ko Kall se nay se	se

Verb (Can) ("နိုင်"Nai)	Conjugate	Translation	Transliteration	Affix
Present Tense	I can read	ငါဖတ်နိုင်သည်	Ngr phat Nai de	de
Past Tense	They could read	သူတို့ဖတ်နိုင်ခဲ့သည်	Thu tot phat Nai ke de	Ke
Future Tense	She is able to read	သူမဖတ်တတ်သည်	Thu ma Nai lame mi	Lame mi
Continuous				

Verb (Choose) ("ရွေးချယ်" Ywe chae)	Conjugate	Translation	Transliteration	Affix
Present Tense	I choose a bag	ငါအိတ်တစ်လုံးရွေးချယ်သည်	Ngr ate ta lone Ywe chae de	de
Past Tense	They chose a hat	သူတို့ဦးထုတ်တစ်လုံးရွေးချယ်ခဲ့သည်	Thu tot ote tote ta lone Ywe cha eke de	Ke
Future Tense	He will choose a racket	သူရက်ကတ်တစ်ချောင်းရွေးချယ်လိမ့်မည်	Thu racket ta chaung Ywe chae lame mi	Lame mi
Continuous	She is choosing lipstick	သူမနှုတ်ခမ်းနီရွေးချယ်ဆဲ	Thu ma na kan ni Ywe chae se	Se

16

Verb (Come) ("လာ" Lar)	Conjugate	Translation	Transliteration	Affix
Present Tense	I come home	ငါအိမ်ပြန်လာသည်	Ngr eain pyan Lar de	de
Past Tense	They came home	သူတို့အိမ်ပြန်လာခဲ့သည်	Thu tot eain pyan Lar ke de	Ke
Future Tense	He will come home	သူအိမ်ပြန်လာလိမ့်မည်	thu eain pyan Lar lame mi	Lame mi
Continuous	She is coming home	သူမအိမ်ပြန်လာနေဆဲ	Thu ma eain pyan Lar nay se	se

Verb (Close) ("ပိတ်" Pate)	Conjugate	Translation	Transliteration	Affix
Present Tense	I close the door	ငါတံခါးပိတ်သည်	Ngar ta kar Pate de	de
Past Tense	They closed the gate	သူတို့ဂိတ်တံခါးပိတ်ခဲ့သည်	Thu tot gate ta kar Pate ke de	Ke
Future Tense	She will close window	သူမပြူတင်းပေါက်ပိတ်လိမ့်မည်	Thu ma pya tin pout Pate lame mi	Lame mi
Continuous	He is closing the shop	သူဆိုင်ကိုပိတ်နေဆဲ	Thu sine ko Pate nay se	se

Verb (Cook) ("ချက်ပြုတ်" Chat pyoute)	Conjugate	Translation	Transliteration	Affix
Present Tense	I cook dinner	ငါညစာချက်ပြုတ်သည်	Ngr nya sar Chat pyoute de	de
Past Tense	They cooked pasta	သူတို့ပါစတာချက်ပြုတ်ခဲ့သည်	Thu tot pasta Chat pyoute ke de	Ke
Future Tense	He will cook pizza	သူပီဇာချက်ပြုတ်လိမ့်မည်	thu pizza Chat pyoute lame mi	Lame mi
Continuous	She is cooking pork	သူမဝက်သားချက်ပြုတ်နေဆဲ	Thu ma wat tar Chat pyoute nay se	se

Verb (Cry) ("ငို" Ngo)	Conjugate	Translation	Transliteration	Affix
Present Tense	I cry at the movie	ငါရုပ်ရှင်ရုံမှာငိုသည်	Ngr yote shin yone mhr Ngo de	de
Past Tense	They cried at home	သူတို့အိမ်မှာငိုခဲ့သည်	Thu tot eain mhr Ngo ke de	Ke
Future Tense	She will cry	သူမငိုလိမ့်မည်	Thu ma Ngo lame mi	Lame mi
Continuous	He is crying	သူငိုနေဆဲ	Thu Ngo nay se	se

Verb (Dance) ("က" Ka)	Conjugate	Translation	Transliteration	Affix
Present Tense	I dance	ငါကသည်	Ngr Ka de	de
Past Tense	They danced	သူတို့ကခဲ့သည်	Thu tot Ka ke de	Ke
Future Tense	She will dance	သူမကလိမ့်မည်	Thu ma Ka lame mi	Lame mi
Continuous	He is dancing	သူကနေဆဲ	Thu Ka nay se	se

Verb (Decide) ("ဆုံးဖြတ်" Sone phat)	Conjugate	Translation	Transliteration	Affix
Present Tense	I decide to dance	ငါကဖို့ဆုံးဖြတ်သည်	Ngr ka po Sone phat de	de
Past Tense	They decided to dace	သူတို့ကဖို့ဆုံးဖြတ်ခဲ့သည်	Thu tot ka po Sone phat ke de	Ke
Future Tense	He will decide to dance	သူကဖို့ဆုံးဖြတ်လိမ့်မည်	Thu ka po Sone phat lame mi	Lame mi
Continuous	She is deciding to dance	သူမကဖို့ဆုံးဖြတ်နေဆဲ	Thu ma ka po Sone phat se	se

Verb (Decrease) ("လျော့" Yot')	Conjugate	Translation	Transliteration	Affix
Present Tense	I decrease the expense	ငါအသုံးစရိတ်ကိုလျော့လိုက်သည်	Ngr atone sayate Yot liede	de
Past Tense	They decreased the speed	သူတို့အရှိန်နှုန်းကိုလျော့ခဲ့သည်	Thu tot ashane nun Yot ke de	Ke
Future Tense	She will decrease her expense	သူမသူမရဲ့အသုံးစရိတ်ကိုလျော့လတ္တံ့	Thu ma atone sayate Yot la tan	La tan
Continuous	He is decreasing the temperature	အဲဒါကအပူချိန်ကိုလျော့နေဆဲ	E dr ka a pu chain ko Yot nay se	se

21

Verb (Die) ("သေဆုံး" Tay sone)	Conjugate	Translation	Transliteration	Affix
Present Tense	I die	ငါသေဆုံးသည်	Ngr Tay sone dee	de
Past Tense	They died yesterday	သူတို့မနေ့ကသေဆုံးခဲ့သည်	Thu tot ma nay kaTay sone ke dee	Ke
Future Tense	I will die in next month	ငါနောက်လသေဆုံးလတ္တံ့	Ngr nout la Tay sone la tan	La tan
Continuous	She is dying	သူမသေဆုံးတော့မည်	Thu ma Tay sone nay dee	Nay

Verb (Do) ("လုပ်" Lote)	Conjugate	Translation	Transliteration	Affix
Present Tense	I do homework	ငါအိမ်စာလုပ်သည်	Ngr eain sar lote dee	de
Past Tense	They did homework	သူတို့အိမ်စာလုပ်ခဲ့သည်	Thu tot eain sar lote ke dee	Ke
Future Tense	She will do homework	သူမအိမ်စာလုပ်လတ္တံ့	Thu ma eain sar lote la tan	La tan
Continuous	He is doing homework	သူအိမ်စာလုပ်ဆဲ	Thu eain sar lote se	se

Verb (Drink) ("သောက်" Tout)	Conjugate	Translation	Transliteration	Affix
Present Tense	I drink water	ငါရေသောက်သည်	Ngr yay Tout dee	de
Past Tense	They drank juice	သူတို့အသီးဖျော်ရည်သောက်ခဲ့သည်	Thu tot a tee pyaw yay Tout ke dee	Ke
Future Tense	She will drink coffee	သူမကော်ဖီသောက်လတ္တံ့	Thu ma koffee Tout la tan	La tan
Continuous	He is drinking tea	သူလက်ဖက်ရည်သောက်နေဆဲ	Thu lapat yay Tout nay se	se

Verb (Drive) ("မောင်း" Mao)	Conjugate	Translation	Transliteration	Affix
Present Tense	I drive	ငါမောင်းသည်	Ngr Mao dee	de
Past Tense	They drove	သူတို့မောင်းခဲ့သည်	Thu tot Mao ke dee	Ke
Future Tense	She will drive	သူမမောင်းလတ္တံ့	Thu ma Mao latan	La tan
Continuous	He is driving	သူမောင်းနေဆဲ	Thu Mao nay se	se

Verb (Eat) ("စား" Sar)	Conjugate	Translation	Transliteration	Affix
Present Tense	I eat pasta	ငါ ပါစတာ စားသည်	Ngr pasta Sar dee	de
Past Tense	They ate rice	သူတို့ထမင်းစားခဲ့သည်	Thu tot tamin Sar ke dee	Ke
Future Tense	She will eat an apple	သူမပန်းသီးစားလတ္တံ့	Thu ma pan tee Sar la tan	La tan
Continuous	He is eating pizza	သူပီဇာစားနေဆဲ	Thu pizar Sar nay se	se

Verb (Enter) ("ဝင်" wan)	Conjugate	Translation	Transliteration	Affix
Present Tense	I enter into the account	ငါအကောင့်ထဲဝင်သည်	Ngr akoun te Wan dee	de
Past Tense	They entered into the home	သူတို့အိမ်ထဲဝင်ခဲ့သည်	Thu tot eain te Wan ke dee	Ke
Future Tense	She will enter into her account	သူမသူမအကောင့်ထဲဝင်လတ္တံ့	Thu ma thu ma akoun te Wan la tan	La tan
Continuous	He is entering into his account	သူသူ့အကောင့်ထဲဝင်နေဆဲ	Thu thu akoun te Wan nay se	se

Verb (Exit) ("ထွက်" htut)	Conjugate	Translation	Transliteration	Affix
Present Tense	I exit from the movie	ငါရုပ်ရှင်ရုံထဲကထွက်သည်	Ngr yote shin yone te ka Htut dee	de
Past Tense	They exited from the movie	သူတို့ရုပ်ရှင်ရုံထဲကထွက်ခဲ့သည်	Thu tot yote shin yone te ka Htut ke dee	Ke
Future Tense	She will exit from the movie	သူမရုပ်ရှင်ရုံထဲကထွက်လတ္တံ့	Thu ma yote shin yone te ka Htut la tan	La tan
Continuous	He is exiting form the movie	သူရုပ်ရှင်ရုံထဲကထွက်နေဆဲ	Thu yote shin yone te ka Htut nay se	se

Verb (Explain) ("ရှင်းပြ" Shin Pya)	Conjugate	Translation	Transliteration	Affix
Present Tense	I explain everything	ငါအကုန်ရှင်းပြသည်	Ngr akone Shin pya dee	de
Past Tense	They explained everything	သူတို့အကုန်ရှင်းပြခဲ့သည်	Thu tot akone Shin pya ke dee	Ke
Future Tense	She will explain anything	သူမဘာမဆိုရှင်းပြလတ္တံ့	Thu ma br maso Shin pya la tan	La tan
Continuous	He is explaining	သူရှင်းပြနေဆဲ	Thu Shin pya Nay se	se

Verb (Fall) ("ပြုတ်ကျ" Pyote Kga)	Conjugate	Translation	Transliteration	Affix
Present Tense	I fall down	ငါပြုတ်ကျသည်	Ngr Pyote kga dee	de
Past Tense	They fell down	သူတို့ပြုတ်ကျခဲ့သည်	Thu tot Pyote kga ke dee	Ke
Future Tense	She will fall down	သူမပြုတ်ကျလိမ့်မည်	Thu ma Pyote kga lame mi	Lame mi
Continuous	She is falling asleep	သူမအိပ်ပျော်နေဆဲ	Thu ma eai pyaw nay se	se

Verb (Feel) ("ခံစား" Khan Sar)	Conjugate	Translation	Transliteration	Affix
Present Tense	I feel sick	ငါနေမကောင်းသလိုခံစားရသည်	Ngr nay ma kaung talo Khan sar ya dee	de
Past Tense	They felt sick	သူတို့နေမကောင်းသလိုခံစားခဲ့ရသည်	Thu tot nay ma kaung talo Khan sar ke ya dee	Ke
Future Tense	She will feel sick	သူမနေမကောင်းသလိုခံစားရလတ္တံ့	Thu ma nay ma kaung talo Khan sar ya la tan	La tan
Continuous	He is feeling sick	သူနေမကောင်းသလိုခံစားရဆဲ	Thu nay ma kaung talo Khan sar ya se	se

Verb (Fight) ("တိုက်ခိုက်" Tai Kai)	Conjugate	Translation	Transliteration	Affix
Present Tense	I fight for freedom	ငါလွတ်လပ်ရေးအတွက်တိုက်ခိုက်သည်	Ngr loot lut yay a twe Tai kai dee	de
Past Tense	They fought for freedom	သူတို့လွတ်လပ်ရေးအတွက်တိုက်ခိုက်ခဲ့သည်	Thu tpt loot lut yay a twe Tai kai ke dee	Ke
Future Tense	She will fight for freedom	သူမလွတ်လပ်ရေးအတွက်တိုက်ခိုက်လတ္တံ့	Thu ma loot lut yay a twe Tai kai la tan	La tan
Continuous	He is fighting for freedom	သူလွတ်လပ်ရေးအတွက်တိုက်ခိုက်ဆဲ	Thu lpot lut yay a twe Tai kai se	se

Verb (Find) ("ရှာတွေ့") Shar twe	Conjugate	Translation	Transliteration	Affix
Present Tense	I find it here	ငါအဲဒါကိုဒီမှာရှာတွေ့သည်	Ngr e dr ko d mr Shar twe dee	de
Past Tense	They found it there	သူတို့အဲဒါကိုဟိုမှာရှာတွေ့ခဲ့သည်	Thu tot e dr ko ho mr Shar twe ke dee	Ke
Future Tense	She will find it there	သူမအဲဒါကိုဟိုမှာရှာတွေ့လတ္တံ့	Thu ma e dr ko ho mr Shar twe la tan	La tan
Continuous	He is finding it here	သူဒီမှာရှာနေဆဲ	Thu d mr Shar nay se	se

Verb (Finish) ("ပြီးဆုံး" Pee Sone)	Conjugate	Translation	Transliteration	Affix
Present Tense	I finish my exam	ငါစာမေးပွဲပြီးဆုံးသည်	Ngr sr may pwe Pee sone dee	de
Past Tense	They finished the exam	သူတို့စာမေးပွဲပြီးဆုံးခဲ့သည်	Thu tot sr may pwe Pee soneke de	Ke
Future Tense	I will finish the exam tomorrow	ငါမနက်ဖြန်စာမေးပွဲပြီးဆုံးလတ္တံ့	Ngr ma nat pyan sr may pwe Pee sone la tan	La tan
Continuous	She is finishing her exam	သူမစာမေးပွဲပြီးဆုံးဆဲ	Thu ma sr may pwe Pee sone se	se

Verb (Fly) ("ပျံသန်း" Pyan tan)	Conjugate	Translation	Transliteration	Affix
Present Tense	I fly to Bangkok	ငါဘန်ကောက်ကိုပျံသန်းသည်	Ngr ban kout ko Pyan tan de	de
Past Tense	They flew to Bangkok	သူတို့ဘန်ကောက်ကိုပျံသန်းခဲ့သည်	Thu tot ban kout ko Pyan tan ke de	Ke
Future Tense	She will fly to New York	သူမနယူးယောက်ကိုပျံသန်းလတ္တံ့	Thu ma nayu youk ko Pyan tan la tan	La tan
Continuous	She is flying to Berlin	သူမဘာလင်ကိုပျံသန်းဆဲ	Thu ma bar lin ko Pyan tan se	se

Verb (Forget) ("မေ့ပျောက်" Maye pyut)	Conjugate	Translation	Transliteration	Affix
Present Tense	I forget her	ငါသူမကိုမေ့ပျောက်သည်	Ngr thu ma ko Maye pyut de	de
Past Tense	They forgot him	သူတို့သူ့ကိုမေ့ပျောက်ခဲ့သည်	Thu tot thu ko Maye pyut ke de	Ke
Future Tense	She will forget him	သူမသူ့ကိုမေ့ပျောက်လတ္တံ့	Thu ma thu ko Maye pyut la tan	La tan
Continuous	He is forgetting her	သူသူမကိုမေ့ပျောက်ဆဲ	Thu thu ma ko Maye pyut se	se

28

Verb (Get up) ("အိပ်ယာထ" eai yar hta)	Conjugate	Translation	Transliteration	Affix
Present Tense	I get up at 6 o'clock	ငါ၆နာရီမှာအိပ်ယာထသည်	Ngr chout na ye mr eai yar Hta de	de
Past Tense	They got up at 6 o'clock	သူတို့၆နာရီမှာအိပ်ယာထခဲ့သည်	Thu tot chout na ye mr eai yar Hta ke de	Ke
Future Tense	She will get up at 6 o'clock	သူမ၆နာရီမှာအိပ်ယာထလတ္တံ့	Thu ma chout na ye mr eai yar Hta la tan	La tan
Continuous	He is getting up at 6 o'clock	သူ၆နာရီမှာအိပ်ယာထနေဆဲ	Thu chout na ye mr eai yar Hta nay se	se

Verb (Give) ("ပေး" Pay)	Conjugate	Translation	Transliteration	Affix
Present Tense	I give away the book	ငါစာအုပ်ကိုပေးသည်	Ngr sar ote Pay de	de
Past Tense	They gave away the book	သူတို့စာအုပ်ကိုပေးခဲ့သည်	Thu tot sar ote Pay ke de	Ke
Future Tense	She will give away the book	သူမစာအုပ်ကိုပေးလတ္တံ့	Thu ma sar ote ko Pay la tan	La tan
Continuous	He is giving away the book	သူစာအုပ်ကိုပေးနေဆဲ	Thu sar ote ko Pay nay se	se

Verb (To go) ("သွား" Twar)	Conjugate	Translation	Transliteration	Affix
Present Tense	I go to school	ငါကျောင်းကိုသွားသည်	Ngr kyaung ko Twar de	de
Past Tense	They went to college	သူတို့ကောလိပ်ကိုသွားခဲ့သည်	Thu to caw leai koTwar ke de	Ke
Future Tense	She will go to university	သူမတက္ကသိုလ်ကိုသွားလတ္တံ	Thu ma takato Twar la tan	La tan
Continuous	He is going to the nursery	သူနေ့ကလေးထိန်းကျောင်းသွားနေဆဲ	Thu nay kalay tain kyaung Twar nay se	se

Verb (Happen) ("ဖြစ်ပွား" Phit puwar)	Conjugate	Translation	Transliteration	Affix
Present Tense	It happens	ဒါဖြစ်ပွားသည်	Dr Phit puwar de	de
Past Tense	They happened to meet him	သူတို့သူကိုတွေ့ဖို့ဖြစ်ပွားခဲ့သည်	Thu to thu ko twe po Phit puwar ke de	Ke
Future Tense	She will happen to meet him	သူမသူကိုတွေ့ဖို့ဖြစ်ပွားလတ္တံ	Thu ma thu ko twe po Phit puwar la tan	La tan
Continuous	It is happening	ဒါဖြစ်ပွားဆဲ	Dr Phit puwar se	se

Verb (Have) ("ရှိ" Shi)	Conjugate	Translation	Transliteration	Affix
Present Tense	I have a cat	ငါ့မှာကြောင်တစ်ကောင်ရှိသည်	Nga mr kyaung ta kaung Shi de	de
Past Tense	They had two dogs	သူတို့မှာခွေးနှစ်ကောင်ရှိခဲ့သည်	Thu to mr kway na kaung Shi ke de	Ke
Future Tense	She will have a turtle	သူမမှာလိပ်တစ်ကောင်ရှိလတ္တံ့	Thu ma mr late ta kaung Shi la tan	La tan
Continuous	He is having a dog	သူမှာခွေးတစ်ကောင်ရှိနေဆဲ	Thu mr kway ta kaung Shi nay se	se

Verb (Hear) ("ကြား"Kyar)	Conjugate	Translation	Transliteration	Affix
Present Tense	I hear	ငါကြားသည်	Ngr Kyar de	de
Past Tense	They heard	ငါကြားခဲ့သည်	Ngr Kyar ke de	Ke
Future Tense	She will hear	သူမကြားလတ္တံ့	Thu ma Kyar la tan	La tan
Continuous	She is hearing	သူမကြားနေဆဲ	Thu ma Kyar nay se	se

Verb (Help) ("ကူညီ" Ku nyi)	Conjugate	Translation	Transliteration	Affix
Present Tense	I help them	ငါသူတို့ကိုကူညီသည်	Ngr thu to ko Ku nyi de	de
Past Tense	They helped her	သူတို့သူမကိုကူညီခဲ့သည်	Thu to thu ma ko Ku nyi ke de	Ke
Future Tense	She will help him	သူမသူ့ကိုကူညီလတ္တံ့	Thu ma thu ko Ku nyi la tan	La tan
Continuous	He is helping her	သူသူမကိုကူညီဆဲ	Thu thu ma ko Ku nyi se	se

Verb (Hold) ("ကိုင်" Gai)	Conjugate	Translation	Transliteration	Affix
Present Tense	I hold the book	ငါစာအုပ်ကိုကိုင်သည်	Ngr sar ote ko Gai de	de
Past Tense	They held the book	သူတို့စာအုပ်ကိုကိုင်ခဲ့သည်	Thu tot sar ote ko Gai ke de	Ke
Future Tense	She will hold the book	သူမစာအုပ်ကိုကိုင်လတ္တံ့	Thu ma sar ote ko Gai la tan	La tan
Continuous	He is holding the shares	သူရှယ်ယာတွေကိုကိုင်နေဆဲ	Thu shae yr twe Gai nay se	se

Verb (Increase) ("တိုး" Toe)	Conjugate	Translation	Transliteration	Affix
Present Tense	I increase my expense	ငါ့ငါ့အသုံးစရိတ်တိုးသည်	Ngr nga atone sayate Toe de	de
Past Tense	They increased the speed	သူတို့အရှိန်တိုးခဲ့သည်	Thu to ashane Toe ke de	Ke
Future Tense	She will increase her usage	သူမသုံးနှုန်းတိုးလတ္တံ့	Thu ma atone sayate Toe la tan	La tan
Continuous	It is increasing	အဲဒါတိုးနေဆဲ	E dar Toe nay se	se

Verb (Introduce) ("မိတ်ဆက်" Mate set)	Conjugate	Translation	Transliteration	Affix
Present Tense	I introduce myself	ငါကိုယ့်ကိုကိုယ်မိတ်ဆက်သည်	Ngr koe ko ko Mate set de	de
Past Tense	They introduced the book	သူတို့စာအုပ်ကိုမိတ်ဆက်ခဲ့သည်	Thu tot sar ote ko Mate set ke de	Ke
Future Tense	She will introduce her book	သူမသူမစာအုပ်ကိုမိတ်ဆက်လတ္တံ့	Thu ma thu ma sar ote ko Mate set la tan	La tan
Continuous	He is introducing his book	သူသူစာအုပ်ကိုမိတ်ဆက်ဆဲ	Thu thu sar ote ko Mate set se	se

Verb (Invite) ("ဖိတ်" Phate)	Conjugate	Translation	Transliteration	Affix
Present Tense	I invite them	ငါသူတို့ကိုဖိတ်သည်	Ngr thu to ko Phate de	de
Past Tense	They invited her	သူတို့သူမကိုဖိတ်ခဲ့သည်	Thu to thu ma ko Phate ke de	Ke
Future Tense	She will invite him	သူမသူ့ကိုဖိတ်လတ္တံ့	Thu ma thu ko Phate la tan	La tan
Continuous	He is inviting her	သူသူမကိုဖိတ်နေဆဲ	Thu thu ma ko Phate nay se	se

Verb (Kill) ("သတ်" Tdat)	Conjugate	Translation	Transliteration	Affix
Present Tense	I kill a worm	ငါတီကောင်တစ်ကောင်ကိုသတ်သည်	Ngr t kaung ta kaung ko Tdat de	de
Past Tense	They killed him	သူတို့သူ့ကိုသတ်ခဲ့သည်	Thu to thu ko Tdat ke de	Ke
Future Tense	She will kill you	သူမမင်းကိုသတ်လတ္တံ့	Thu ma min ko tdat la tan	La tan
Continuous	He is killing a worm	သူတီကောင်တစ်ကောင်ကိုသတ်နေဆဲ	Thu t kaung ta kaung ko Tdat nay se	se

Verb (Kiss) ("နမ်း" Nam)	Conjugate	Translation	Transliteration	Affix
Present Tense	I kiss a rose	ငါနှင်းဆီတစ်ပွင့်ကိုနမ်းသည်	Ngr nin se ta pwin ko Nam de	de
Past Tense	They kissed the roses	သူတို့နှင်းဆီတွေကိုနမ်းခဲ့သည်	Thu to nin se twe ko Nam ke de	Ke
Future Tense	She will kiss the rose	သူမနှင်းဆီပန်းကိုနမ်းလတ္တံ့	Thu ma nin se pan ko Nam la tan	La tan
Continuous	He is kissing roses	သူနှင်းဆီတွေကိုနမ်းနေဆဲ	Thu nin se twe ko Nam nay se	se

Verb (Know) ("သိ" Ti)	Conjugate	Translation	Transliteration	Affix
Present Tense	I know you	ငါမင်းကိုသိသည်	၊ Ngr min ko Ti de	de
Past Tense	They knew you	သူတို့မင်းကိုသိခဲ့သည်	၊ Thu to min ko Ti ke de	Ke
Future Tense	She will know you	သူမမင်းကိုသိလတ္တံ့	၊ ⸜ Thu ma min ko Ti la tan	La tan
Continuous	He is knowing you	သူမင်းကိုသိနေဆဲ	၊ Thu min ko Ti nay se	se

Verb (Laugh) ("ရယ်မော" Yee maw)	Conjugate	Translation	Transliteration	Affix
Present Tense	I laugh	ငါရယ်မောသည်	Ngr Yee maw de	de
Past Tense	They laughed	သူတို့ရယ်မောခဲ့သည်	Thu to Yee maw ke de	Ke
Future Tense	She will laugh	သူမရယ်မောလတ္တံ့	၊ Thu ma Yee maw la tan	La tan
Continuous	He is laughing	သူရယ်မောဆဲ	Thu Yee maw se	se

Verb (Learn) ("လေ့လာ" Lae lar)	Conjugate	Translation	Transliteration	Affix
Present Tense	I learn a lesson	ငါသင်ခန်းစာတစ်ခုလေ့လာသည်	Ngr tin kan sar ta ku Lae lar de	de
Past Tense	They learned a lesson	သူတို့သင်ခန်းစာတစ်ခုလေ့လာခဲ့သည်	Thu to tin kan sar ta ku Lae lar ke de	Ke
Future Tense	She will learn a lesson	သူမသင်ခန်းစာတစ်ခုလေ့လာလတ္တံ့	Thu ma tin kan sar ta ku Lae lar la tan	La tan
Continuous	He is learning a lesson	သူမသင်ခန်းစာတစ်ခုလေ့လာဆဲ	Thu ma tin kan sar ta ku Lae lar se	se

Verb (Lie down) ("လှဲလျောင်း" Lea laung)	Conjugate	Translation	Transliteration	Affix
Present Tense	I lie down on the floor	ငါကြမ်းပြင်ပေါ်လှဲလျောင်းသည်	Ngr kyan pyin paw Lea laung de	de
Past Tense	They lay down on the floor	သူတို့ကြမ်းပြင်ပေါ်လှဲလျောင်းခဲ့သည်	Thu to kyan pyin paw Lea laung ke de	Ke
Future Tense	She will lie down on the floor	သူမကြမ်းပြင်ပေါ်လှဲလျောင်းလတ္တံ့	Thu ma kyan pyin paw Lea laung la tan	La tan
Continuous	He is lying down on the floor	သူကြမ်းပြင်ပေါ်လှဲလျောင်းဆဲ	Thu kyan pyin paw Lea laung se	se

Myanmar Language: 101 Burmese Verbs

Verb (Like) ("ကြိုက်" Kyite)	Conjugate	Translation	Transliteration	Affix
Present Tense	I like to eat	ငါစားရတာကြိုက်သည်	Ngr sar ya tr Kyite de	de
Past Tense	They liked to drink	သူတို့သောက်ရတာကြိုက်ခဲ့သည်	Thu to thou ya tr Kyite ke de	Ke
Future Tense	She will like to dance	သူမကရတာကြိုက်လတ္တံ့	Thu ma ka ya tr Kyite la tan	La tan
Continuous	He likes dancing	သူကရတာကိုကြိုက်နေဆဲ	Thu ka ya tar ko Kyite nay se	se

Verb (Listen) ("နားထောင်" Nar htaung)	Conjugate	Translation	Transliteration	Affix
Present Tense	I listen to music	ငါသီချင်းနားထောင်သည်	Ngr te chin Nar htaung de	de
Past Tense	They listened to a song	သူတို့သီချင်းတစ်ပုဒ်နားထောင်ခဲ့သည်	Thu to te chin ta pote Nar htaung ke de	Ke
Future Tense	She will listen to a song	သူမသီချင်းတစ်ပုဒ်နားထောင်လတ္တံ့	Thu ma te chin ta pote Nar htaung la tan	La tan
Continuous	He is listening to a song	သူသီချင်းတစ်ပုဒ်နားထောင်ဆဲ	Thu te chin ta pote Nar htaung se	se

Verb (Live) ("နေထိုင်" Nay htai)	Conjugate	Translation	Transliteration	Affix
Present Tense	I live in Myanmar	ငါမြန်မာပြည်မှာနေထိုင်သည်	Ngr Myanmar pye mr Nay htai de	de
Past Tense	They lived in Yangon	သူတို့ရန်ကုန်မှာနေထိုင်ခဲ့သည်	Thu to Yangon mr Nay htai ke de	Ke
Future Tense	She will live in Myanmar	သူမမြန်မာပြည်မှာနေထိုင်လတ္တံ့	Thu ma Myanmar pye mr Nay htai la tan	La tan
Continuous	He is living in Yangon	သူရန်ကုန်မှာနေထိုင်ဆဲ	Thu Yangon mr Nay htai se	se

Verb (Loose) ("ဖြုတ်" Phyote)	Conjugate	Translation	Transliteration	Affix
Present Tense	I loose the buttons	ငါကြယ်သီးတွေကိုဖြုတ်သည်	Ngr kye te twe ko Phyote de	de
Past Tense	They loosed the buttons	သူတို့ကြယ်သီးတွေကိုဖြုတ်ခဲ့သည်	Thu to kye te twe ko Phyote ke de	Ke
Future Tense	She will loose the buttons	သူမကြယ်သီးတွေကိုဖြုတ်လတ္တံ့	Thu ma kye te twe ko Phyote la'tan	La tan
Continuous	He is loosing the buttons	သူကြယ်သီးတွေကိုဖြုတ်နေဆဲ	Thu kye te twe ko Phyote nay se	se

Verb (Love) ("ချစ်" Chit) ("ကြိုက်" Kyite)	Conjugate	Translation	Transliteration	Affix
Present Tense	I love to eat	ငါစားရတာကိုကြိုက်သည်	Ngr sar ya tr ko Kyite de	de
Past Tense	They loved to drink	သူတို့သောက်ရတာကိုကြိုက်ခဲ့သည်	Thu to sar ya tr ko Kyite ke de	Ke
Future Tense	He will love to dance	သူကရတာကိုကြိုက်လတ္တံ့	Thu ka ya tr ko Kyite la tan	La tan
Continuous	She is loving dancing	သူမကရတာကိုကြိုက်နေဆဲ	Thu ma ka ya tr ko Kyite nay se	se

Verb (Meet) ("တွေ့ဆုံ" Tawe sone)	Conjugate	Translation	Transliteration	Affix
Present Tense	I meet you	ငါမင်းကိုတွေ့ဆုံသည်	Ngr min ko Tawe sone de	de
Past Tense	They met me	သူတို့ငါ့ကိုတွေ့ဆုံခဲ့သည်	Thu to nga ko Tawe son eke de	Ke
Future Tense	She will meet you	သူမမင်းကိုတွေ့ဆုံလတ္တံ့	Thu ma min ko Tawe sone la tan	La tan
Continuous	He is meeting her	သူသူမကိုတွေ့ဆုံဆဲ	Thu thu ma ko Tawe sone se	se

39

Verb (Need) ("လိုအပ်" Lo app)	Conjugate	Translation	Transliteration	Affix
Present Tense	I need to sleep	ငါအိပ်ဖို့လိုအပ်သည်	Ngr eai po Lo app de	de
Past Tense	They needed to eat	သူတို့စားဖို့လိုအပ်ခဲ့သည်	Thu to sar po Lo app ke de	Ke
Future Tense	She will need to eat	သူမစားဖို့လိုအပ်လတ္တံ့	Thu ma sar po Lo app la tan	La tan
Continuous	He is needing to sleep	သူအိပ်ဖို့လိုအပ်ဆဲ	Thu ate po Lo app se	se

Verb (Notice) ("သတိပြု" Ta di pyu)	Conjugate	Translation	Transliteration	Affix
Present Tense	I notice her	ငါသူမကိုသတိပြုမိသည်	Ngr thu ma ko Ta di pyu mi de	de
Past Tense	They noticed me	သူတို့ငါ့ကိုသတိပြုမိခဲ့သည်	Thu to Nga ko Ta di pyu mi ke de	Ke
Future Tense	She will notice you	သူမမင်းကိုသတိပြုမိလတ္တံ့	Thu ma min ko Ta di pyu mi la tan	La tan
Continuous	He is noticing her	သူသူမကိုသတိပြုမိဆဲ	Thu thu ma ko Ta di pyu mi se	se

Verb (Open) ("ဖွင့်" Phuet)	Conjugate	Translation	Transliteration	Affix
Present Tense	I open the shop	ငါဆိုင်ဖွင့်သည်	Ngr sai Phuet de	de
Past Tense	They opened the shop	သူတို့ဆိုင်ဖွင့်ခဲ့သည်	Thu to sai Phuet ke de	Ke
Future Tense	She will open the shop	သူမဆိုင်ဖွင့်လတ္တံ့	Thu ma sai Phuet la tan	La tan
Continuous	He is opening the shop	သူဆိုင်ဖွင့်နေဆဲ	Thu sai Phuet nay se	se

Verb (Play) ("ကစား" Ka sar)	Conjugate	Translation	Transliteration	Affix
Present Tense	I play games	ငါဂိမ်းကစားသည်	Ngr gane Ka sar de	de
Past Tense	They played football	သူတို့ဘောလုံးကစားခဲ့သည်	Thu to baw lone Ka sar ke de	Ke
Future Tense	She will play tennis	သူမတင်းနစ်ကစားလတ္တံ့	Thu ma tin nit Ka sar la tan	La tan
Continuous	He is playing tennis	သူမတင်းနစ်ကစားဆဲ	Thu ma tin nit Ka sar se	se

Verb (Put) ("ထည့်" the)	Conjugate	Translation	Transliteration	Affix
Present Tense	I put the money in the can	ငါဘူးထဲမှာပိုက်ဆံထည့်ထားသည်	Ngr buu Hte mr pite san hte Htar de	de
Past Tense	They put the money in the can	သူတို့ဘူးထဲမှာပိုက်ဆံထည့်ထားခဲ့သည်	Thu to buu hte mr pite san hte Htar ke de	Ke
Future Tense	She will put the money in the can	သူမဘူးထဲမှာပိုက်ဆံထည့်ထားလတ္တံ့	Thu ma buu hte mr pite san hte Htar la tan	La tan
Continuous	He is putting the money in the can	သူဘူးထဲမှာပိုက်ဆံထည့်ထားနေဆဲ	Thu buu hte mr pite san hte Htar nay se	se

Verb (Read) ("ဖတ်" Phat)	Conjugate	Translation	Transliteration	Affix
Present Tense	I read a book	ငါစာအုပ်တစ်အုပ်ဖတ်သည်	Ngr Sar ote ta ote Phat de	de
Past Tense	They read a letter	သူတို့စာတစ်စောင်ဖတ်ခဲ့သည်	Thu to Sar ta saung Phat ke de	Ke
Future Tense	She will read a book	သူမစာအုပ်တစ်အုပ်ဖတ်လတ္တံ့	Thu ma Sar ote ta ote Phat la tan	La tan
Continuous	He is reading a letter	သူစာတစ်စောင်စာဖတ်ဆဲ	Thu Sar ta saung Phat se	se

Verb (Receive) ("လက်ခံ" Lat kan)	Conjugate	Translation	Transliteration	Affix
Present Tense	I receive mail	ငါချောပို့တစ်ခုလက်ခံသည်	Ngr chaw po ta ku Lat kan de	de
Past Tense	They received mail	သူတို့ပို့ချောပို့တစ်ခုလက်ခံခဲ့သည်	Thu to chaw po ta ku Lat kan ke de	Ke
Future Tense	He will receive mail	သူချောပို့တစ်ခုလက်ခံလတ္တံ့	Thu ma chaw po ta ku Lat kan la tan	La tan
Continuous	She is receiving mail	သူမချောပို့တစ်ခုလက်ခံဆဲ	Thu ma chaw po ta ku Lat kan se	se

Verb (Remember) ("သတိရ") ta di ya)	Conjugate	Translation	Transliteration	Affix
Present Tense	I remember her	ငါသူမကိုသတိရသည်	Ngr thu ma ko ta di ya de	de
Past Tense	They remembered her	သူတို့သူမကိုသတိရခဲ့သည်	Thu to thu ma ko Ta di yak e de	Ke
Future Tense	She will remember him	သူမသူ့ကိုသတိရလတ္တံ့	Thu ma thu ko Ta di ya la tan	La tan
Continuous	She is remembering him	သူမသူ့ကိုသတိရဆဲ	Thu ma thu ko Ta di ya se	se

Verb (Repeat) ("ထပ်ခါလုပ်" Htet khar lote)	Conjugate	Translation	Transliteration	Affix
Present Tense	I repeat the exercises	ငါလေ့ကျင့်ခန်းတွေကိုထပ်ခါလုပ်သည်	Ngr lay kyint kan twe ko Htet khar lote de	de
Past Tense	They repeated the exercise	သူတို့လေ့ကျင့်ခန်းတွေကိုထပ်ခါလုပ်ခဲ့သည်	Thu₁ to lay kyint kan twe ko Htet khar lot eke de	Ke
Future Tense	She will repeat the exercise	သူမလေ့ကျင့်ခန်းတွေကိုထပ်ခါလုပ်လတ္တံ့	Thu ma lay kyint kan twe ko Htet khar lote la tan	La tan
Continuous	He is repeating the exercise	သူလေ့ကျင့်ခန်းတွေကိုထပ်ခါလုပ်ဆဲ	Thu ma lay kyint kan twe ko Htet khar lote se	se

Verb (Return) ("ပြန်လာ" Pyan lar)	Conjugate	Translation	Transliteration	Affix
Present Tense	I return home	ငါအိမ်ပြန်လာသည်	Ngr eain Pyan lar de	de
Past Tense	They returned home	သူတို့အိမ်ကိုပြန်လာခဲ့သည်	Thu to eain ko Pyan lar ke de	Ke
Future Tense	She will return home	သူမအိမ်ကိုပြန်လာလတ္တံ့	Thu ma eain ko Pyan lar là tan	La tan
Continuous	He is returning home	သူအိမ်ကိုပြန်လာဆဲ	Thu eain ko Pyan lar se	se

44

Verb (Run) ("ေျပး" Pyay)	Conjugate	Translation	Transliteration	Affix
Present Tense	I run	ငါေျပးသည်	Ngr Pyay de	de
Past Tense	They ran	သူတို့ေျပးခဲ့သည်	Thu to Pyay ke de	Ke
Future Tense	She will run	သူမေျပးလတ္တံ့	| Thu ma Pyay la tan	La tan
Continuous	He is running	သူေျပးေနဆဲ	Thu Pyay nay se	se

Verb (Say) ("ေျပာ" Pyawr)	Conjugate	Translation	Transliteration	Affix
Present Tense	I say	ငါေျပာသည်	Ngr Pyawr de	de
Past Tense	They said	သူတို့ေျပာခဲ့သည်	Thu to Pyawr ke de	Ke
Future Tense	She will say	သူမေျပာလတ္တံ့	| Thu ma Pyawr la tan	La tan
Continuous	He is saying	သူေျပာေနဆဲ	Thu Pyawr nay se	se

Verb (Scream) ("ေအာ်" Aww)	Conjugate	Translation	Transliteration	Affix
Present Tense	I scream	ငါေအာ်သည်	Ngr Aww de	de
Past Tense	They screamed	သူတို့ေအာ်ခဲ့သည်	Thu to Aww ke de	Ke
Future Tense	She will scream	သူမေအာ်လတ္တံ့	| Thu ma Aww la tan	La tan
Continuous	He is screaming	သူေအာ်ေနဆဲ	Thu Aww nay se	se

45

Verb (See) ("ေတွ့" twe)	Conjugate	Translation	Transliteration	Affix
Present Tense	I see a cow	ငါနွားတစ်ကောင်တွေ့သည်	Ngr Nwr ta kg twe de	de
Past Tense	They saw a cow	သူတို့နွားတစ်ကောင်တွေ့ခဲ့သည်	Thu tot Nwr ta kg twe ke de	Ke
Future Tense	She will see a cow	သူမနွားတစ်ကောင်တွေ့လတ္တံ့	Thu ma Nwr ta kg twe la tan	La tan
Continuous	He is seeing doctor	သူဆရာဝင်နဲ့တွေ့နေဆဲ	Thu saya wun ne twe nay se	se

Verb (Seem) ("ပုံေပါ်" Pone paw	Conjugate	Translation	Transliteration	Affix
Present Tense	I seem to be tired	ငါပင်ပန်းနေပုံပေါ်သည်	Ngr pin pan nay Pone paw de	de
Past Tense	They seemed to be tired	သူတို့ပင်ပန်းနေပုံပေါ်ခဲ့သည်	Thu tot pin pan nay Pone paw ke de	Ke
Future Tense	She will seem to be tired	သူမပင်ပန်းနေပုံပေါ်လတ္တံ့	Thu ma pin pan nay Pone paw la tan	La tan
Continuous	He is seeming tired	သူပင်ပန်းနေပုံပေါ်နေဆဲ	Thu pin pan nay Pone paw se	se

Verb (Sell) ("ရောင်းချ" Yaung cha)	Conjugate	Translation	Transliteration	Affix
Present Tense	I sell a phone	ငါဖုန်းတစ်လုံးရောင်းချသည်	Ngr fone ta lone Yaung cha de	de
Past Tense	They sold a phone	သူတို့ဖုန်းတစ်လုံးရောင်းချခဲ့သည်	Thu to fone ta lone Yaung cha ke de	Ke
Future Tense	She will sell a phone	သူမဖုန်းတစ်လုံးရောင်းချလတ္တံ့	Thu ma fone ta lone Yaung cha la tan	La tan
Continuous	He is selling a phone	သူဖုန်းတစ်လုံးရောင်းချဆဲ	Thu fone ta lone Yaung cha se	se

Verb (Send) ("ပို့" Poe)	Conjugate	Translation	Transliteration	Affix
Present Tense	I send mail	ငါချောပို့တစ်ခုပို့သည်	Ngr chaw po ta ku Poe de	de
Past Tense	They sent mail	သူတို့ချောပို့တစ်ခုပို့ခဲ့သည်	Thu tot chaw po ta ku Poe ke de	Ke
Future Tense	She will send mail	သူမချောပို့တစ်ခုပို့လတ္တံ့	Thu ma chaw po ta ku Poe la tan	La tan
Continuous	He is sending mail	သူချောပို့တစ်ခုပို့နေဆဲ	Thu chaw po ta ku Poe nay se	se

Verb (Show) ("ပြသ" Pyar tha)	Conjugate	Translation	Transliteration	Affix
Present Tense	I show mail	ငါချောပို့တစ်ခုပြသသည်	Ngr Chaw po ta ku Pyar tha de	de
Past Tense	They showed mail	သူတို့ချောပို့တစ်ခုပြသခဲ့သည်	Thu tot chaw po ta ku Pyar tha ke de	Ke
Future Tense	She will show mail	သူမချောပို့တစ်ခုပြသလတ္တံ့	Thu ma chaw po ta ku Pyar tha la tan	La tan
Continuous	He is showing mail	သူချောပို့တစ်ခုပြသဆဲ	Thu ma chaw po ta ku Pyar tha se	se

Verb (Sing) ("သီဆို" Ti so)	Conjugate	Translation	Transliteration	Affix
Present Tense	I sing a song	ငါသီချင်းတစ်ပုဒ်သီဆိုသည်	Ngr te chin ta pote Ti so de	de
Past Tense	They sang a song	သူတို့သီချင်းတစ်ပုဒ်သီဆိုခဲ့သည်	Thu to te chin ta pote Ti so ke de	Ke
Future Tense	He will sing a song	သူသီချင်းတစ်ပုဒ်သီဆိုလတ္တံ့	Thu te chin ta pote Ti so la tan	La tan
Continuous	She is singing a song	သူမသီချင်းတစ်ပုဒ်သီဆိုဆဲ	Thu ma te chin ta pote Ti so se	se

Verb (Sit down) ("ထိုင်ချ" Htai cha)	Conjugate	Translation	Transliteration	Affix
Present Tense	I sit down on a chair	ငါထိုင်ခုံတစ်ခုပေါ်ထိုင်ချသည်	Ngr tine kone ta ku paw ＼ Htai cha de	de
Past Tense	They sat down on a chair	သူတို့ထိုင်ခုံတစ်ခုပေါ်ထိုင်ချခဲ့သည်	Thu to tine kone ta ku ＼ paw Htai cha ke de	Ke
Future Tense	She will sit down on a chair	သူမထိုင်ခုံတစ်ခုပေါ်ထိုင်ချလတ္တံ့	Thu ma tine kone ta ku ＼ ∣ paw Htai cha la tan	La tan
Continuous	He is sitting down on a chair	သူထိုင်ခုံတစ်ခုပေါ်ထိုင်ချနေဆဲ	Thu tine kone ta ku paw ＼ Htai cha se	se

Verb (Sleep) ("အိပ်" Eaì)	Conjugate	Translation	Transliteration	Affix
Present Tense	I sleep	ငါအိပ်သည်	＼ Ngr Eai de	de
Past Tense	They slept	သူတို့အိပ်ခဲ့သည်	＼ Thu to Eai ke de	Ke
Future Tense	She will sleep	သူမအိပ်လတ္တံ့	＼ ∣ Thu ma Eai la tan	La tan
Continuous	He is sleeping	သူအိပ်နေဆဲ	＼ Thu Eai nay se	se

Verb (Smile) ("ပြုံး" Pyone)	Conjugate	Translation	Transliteration	Affix
Present Tense	I smile	ငါပြုံးသည်	Ngr Pyone de	de
Past Tense	They smiled	သူတို့ပြုံးခဲ့သည်	Thu to Pyone ke de	Ke
Future Tense	She will smile	သူမပြုံးလတ္တံ့	Thu ma Pyone la tan	La tan
Continuous	He is smiling	သူပြုံးနေဆဲ	Thu Pyone nay se	se

Verb (Speak) ("ပြော" Pywar)	Conjugate	Translation	Transliteration	Affix
Present Tense	I speak Burmese	ငါမြန်မာစကားပြောသည်	Ngr Myanmar Sa kar pywar de	de
Past Tense	They spoke Burmese	သူမမြန်မာစကားပြောခဲ့သည်	Thu ma Myanmar Sa kar pywar ke de	Ke
Future Tense	She will speak Burmese	သူမမြန်မာစကားပြောလတ္တံ့	Thu ma Myanmar Sa kar pywar la tan	La tan
Continuous	He is speaking Burmese	သူမြန်မာစကားပြောဆဲ	Thu Myanmar Sa kar pywar se	se

Verb (Stand) ("ရပ်တည်" Yet dti)	Conjugate	Translation	Transliteration	Affix
Present Tense	I stand	ငါရပ်တည်သည်	Ngr Yet dti de	de
Past Tense	They stood	သူတို့ရပ်တည်ခဲ့သည်	Thu to Yet dti ke de	Ke
Future Tense	She will stand	သူမရပ်တည်လတ္တံ့	Thu ma Yet dti la tan	La tan
Continuous	He is standing	သူရပ်တည်ဆဲ	Thu Yet dti se	se

Verb (Start) ("စတင်" Sa tin)	Conjugate	Translation	Transliteration	Affix
Present Tense	I start the race	ငါပြိုင်ပွဲကိုစတင်သည်	Ngr pyai pwe ko Sa tin de	de
Past Tense	They started the race	သူတို့ပြိုင်ပွဲကိုစတင်ခဲ့သည်	Thu tot pyai pwe ko Sa tin ke de	Ke
Future Tense	She will start the race	သူမပြိုင်ပွဲကိုစတင်လိမ့်မည်	Thu ma pyai pwe ko Sa tin lame mi	La tan
Continuous	He is starting the race	သူပြိုင်ပွဲကိုစတင်ဆဲ	Thu pyai pwe ko Sa tin se	se

Verb (Stay) ("နေ" Nay)	Conjugate	Translation	Transliteration	Affix
Present Tense	Istay at a hotel	ငါ ဟိုတယ်တွင် နေသည်	Nga Hotel twin Nay de	de
Past Tense	They stayed at a hotel	သူတို့ ဟိုတယ်တွင် နေခဲ့သည်	Thu doe Hotel twin Nay ke di	Ke
Future Tense	She will stay at a hotel	သူမ ဟိုတယ်တွင် နေလတ္တံ့	Thu ma| Hotel twin Nay la tan	La tan
Continuous	He is staying at a hotel	သူ ဟိုတယ်တွင် နေနေဆဲ	Thu Hotel twin Nay nay se	se

Verb (Take) ("ယူ" Yu	Conjugate	Translation	Transliteration	Affix
Present Tense	I take picture	ငါဓာတ်ပုံရိုက်ယူသည်	Ngr dat pone yai Yu de	de
Past Tense	They took picture	သူတို့ဓာတ်ပုံရိုက်ယူခဲ့သည်	Thu tot dat pone yai Yu ke de	Ke
Future Tense	She will take picture	သူမဓာတ်ပုံရိုက်ယူလတ္တံ့	Thu ma dat pone yai Yu	la tan	La tan
Continuous	He is taking picture	သူဓာတ်ပုံရိုက်ယူနေဆဲ	Thu dat pone yai Yu nay se	se

Verb (Talk) ("ဆွေးနွေး" Swe nawe)	Conjugate	Translation	Transliteration	Affix
Present Tense	I talk to him	ငါသူနဲ့ဆွေးနွေးသည်	Ngr thu ne Swe nawe de	de
Past Tense	They talked to him	သူတို့သူနဲ့ဆွေးနွေးခဲ့သည်	Thu to thu ne Swe nawe ke de	Ke
Future Tense	She will talk to him	သူမသူနဲ့ဆွေးနွေးလတ္တံ့	Thu ma thu ne Swe nawe la tan	La tan
Continuous	He is talking to him	သူသူနဲ့ဆွေးနွေးဆဲ	Thu thu ne Swe nawe se	se

Verb (Teach) ("သင်ကြား" Tin kyar)	Conjugate	Translation	Transliteration	Affix
Present Tense	I teach Burmese	ငါမြန်မာစာသင်ကြားသည်	Ngr Myanmar sar Tin kyar de	de
Past Tense	They taught Burmese	သူတို့မြန်မာစာသင်ကြားခဲ့သည်	Thu to Myanmar sar Tin kyar ke de	Ke
Future Tense	She will teach Burmese	သူမမြန်မာစာသင်ကြားလတ္တံ့	Thu ma Myanmar sar Tin kyar la tan	La tan
Continuous	He is teaching Burmese	သူမြန်မာစာသင်ကြားဆဲ	Thu Myanmar sar Tin kyar se	se

Verb (Think) ("စဉ်းစား" Sin sar)	Conjugate	Translation	Transliteration	Affix
Present Tense	I think twice	ငါနှစ်ခါစဉ်းစားသည်	Ngr na khrSin sar de	de
Past Tense	They though twice	သူတို့နှစ်ခါစဉ်းစားခဲ့သည်	Thu to na khr Sin sar ke de	Ke
Future Tense	He will think twice	သူနှစ်ခါစဉ်းစားလတ္တံ့	၊ Thu na khr Sin sar la tan	La tan
Continuous	She is thinking twice	သူမနှစ်ခါစဉ်းစားဆဲ	Thu ma na khr Sin sar se	se

Verb (Touch) ("ထိ" Hti)	Conjugate	Translation	Transliteration	Affix
Present Tense	I touch her hands	ငါသူမလက်တွေကိုထိမိသည်	၊ Ngr thu ma lat twe ko Hti ၊ mi de	de
Past Tense	They touch her hands	သူတို့သူမလက်တွေကိုထိမိခဲ့သည်	Thu to thu ma lat twe ko ၊ ၊ Hti mi ke de	Ke
Future Tense	She will touch her hands	သူမသူမလက်တွေကိုထိမိလတ္တံ့	Thu ma thu ma lat twe ၊ ၊ ၊ ko Hti mi la tan	La tan
Continuous	He is touching her hands	သူသူလက်တွေကိုထိမိနေဆဲ	၊ ၊ Thu thu lat twe ko Hti mi nay se	se

Verb (Travel) ("ခရီးသွား" Kay ii twar)	Conjugate	Translation	Transliteration	Affix
Present Tense	Travel to Yangon	ရန်ကုန်ကိုခရီးသွားသည်	Yangon ko Ka yii twar de	de
Past Tense	She travelled to Yangon	သူမရန်ကုန်ကိုခရီးသွားခဲ့သည်	Thu ma Yangon ko Ka yii twar ke de	Ke
Future Tense	They will travel to Yangon	သူတို့ရန်ကုန်ကိုခရီးသွားလတ္တံ့	Thu to Yangon ko Ka yii / twar la tan	La tan
Continuous	He is traveling to Yangon	သူရန်ကုန်ကိုခရီးသွားဆဲ	Thu Yangon ko Ka yii twar se	se

Verb (Understand) ("နားလည်" Nar lae)	Conjugate	Translation	Transliteration	Affix
Present Tense	She understands you	သူမမင်းကိုနားလည်သည်	Thu ma min ko Nar lae de	de
Past Tense	I understood you	ငါမင်းကိုနားလည်ခဲ့သည်	Ngr min ko Nar laeke de	Ke
Future Tense	They will understand you	သူတို့မင်းကိုနားလည်လတ္တံ့	Thu to min ko Nar lae la tan	La tan
Continuous	He is understanding you	သူမင်းကိုနားလည်ဆဲ	Thu min ko Nar lae se	se

Verb (Use) ("အသုံးပြု" Ar tone pyu)	Conjugate	Translation	Transliteration	Affix
Present Tense	She uses bathroom	သူမအိမ်သာအသုံးပြုသည်	Thu ma Eain thr Ar tone pyu de	de
Past Tense	I used bathroom	ငါအိမ်သာအသုံးပြုခဲ့သည်	Ngr eain thr Ar tone pyu ke de	Ke
Future Tense	They will use bathroom	သူတို့အိမ်သာအသုံးပြုလတ္တံ့	Thu to eain thr Ar tone pyu la tan	La tan
Continuous	He is using bathroom	သူအိမ်သာအသုံးပြုဆဲ	Thu Ar tone pyu se	se

Verb (Wait) ("စောင့်" Saung)	Conjugate	Translation	Transliteration	Affix
Present Tense	I wait for you	ငါမင်းကိုစောင့်သည်	Ngr min ko Saung de	de
Past Tense	They waited for you	သူတို့မင်းကိုစောင့်ခဲ့သည်	Thu to min ko Saung ke de	Ke
Future Tense	She will wait for you	သူမမင်းကိုစောင့်လတ္တံ့	Thu ma min ko Saung la tan	La tan
Continuous	He is waiting for you	သူမင်းကိုစောင့်နေဆဲ	Thu min ko Saung nay se	se

Verb (Walk) ("လမ်းလျှောက်" lan Shout)	Conjugate	Translation	Transliteration	Affix
Present Tense	I walk	ငါလမ်းလျှောက်သည်	Ngr lan Shout de	de
Past Tense	She walked	သူမလမ်းလျှောက်ခဲ့သည်	Thu ma lan Shout ke de	Ke
Future Tense	They will walk	သူတို့လမ်းလျှောက်လတ္တံ့	\ Thu to lan Shout la tan	La tan
Continuous	He is walking	သူလမ်းလျှောက်နေဆဲ	Thu lan Shout nay se	se

Verb (Want) ("(လို)ချင်" (lo) chin	Conjugate	Translation	Transliteration	Affix
Present Tense	I want to eat	ငါစားချင်သည်	Ngr sar chin de	de
Past Tense	She wanted to eat	သူမစားချင်ခဲ့သည်	Thu ma sar chin ke de	Ke
Future Tense	They will want to eat	သူတို့စားချင်လတ္တံ့	\ Thu to sar chin la tan	La tan
Continuous	He is wanting to eat	သူစားချင်နေဆဲ	Thu sar chin se	se

Verb (Watch) ("ကြည့်" Kyi)	Conjugate	Translation	Transliteration	Affix
Present Tense	She watches a movie	သူမရုပ်ရှင်တစ်ကားကြည့်သည်	Thu ma yote shin ta kar kyi de	de
Past Tense	I watched a movie	ငါရုပ်ရှင်တစ်ကားကြည့်ခဲ့သည်	Ngr yote shin ta kar kyi ke de	Ke
Future Tense	They will watch a movie	သူတို့ရုပ်ရှင်တစ်ကားကြည့်လတ္တံ့	Thu tot yote shin ta kar \ kyi la tan	La tan
Continuous	He is watching a movie	သူရုပ်ရှင်တစ်ကားကြည့်ဆဲ	Thu yote shin ta kar kyi se	se

Verb (Win) ("အောင်နိုင်" Aung nai)	Conjugate	Translation	Transliteration	Affix
Present Tense	I win	ငါအောင်နိုင်သည်	Ngr Aung nai de	de
Past Tense	She won	သူမအောင်နိုင်ခဲ့သည်	Thu ma Aung nai ke de	Ke
Future Tense	They will win	သူတို့အောင်နိုင်လတ္တံ့	Thu to Aung nai la tan	La tan
Continuous	He is winning	သူအောင်နိုင်ဆဲ	Thu Aung nai se	se

Verb (Work) ("အလုပ်" Ar lote)	Conjugate	Translation	Transliteration	Affix
Present Tense	I work	ငါအလုပ်ဖြစ်သည်	Ngr Ar lote phit de	de
Past Tense	He worked	သူအလုပ်ဖြစ်ခဲ့သည်	Thu Ar lote phit ke de	Ke
Future Tense	She will work	သူမအလုပ်ဖြစ်လတ္တံ့	Thu ma Ar lote phit la tan	La tan
Continuous	They are working	သူတို့အလုပ်ဖြစ်ဆဲ	Thu to Ar lote phit se	se

Verb (Write) ("ရေးသား" Yae thar)	Conjugate	Translation	Transliteration	Affix
Present Tense	I write a letter	ငါစာတစ်စောင်ရေးသားသည်	Ngr sar ta saung Yae thar de	de
Past Tense	He wrote a letter	သူစာတစ်စောင်ရေးသားခဲ့သည်	Thu sar ta saung Yae thar ke de	Ke
Future Tense	She will write a letter	သူမစာတစ်စောင်ရေးသားလတ္တံ့	Thu ma sar ta saung Yae ၊ thar la tan	La tan
Continuous	They are writing a letter	သူတို့စာတစ်စောင်ရေးသားဆဲ	Thu to sar ta saung Yae thar se	se

www.ingramcontent.com/pod-product-compliance
Lightning Source LLC
Chambersburg PA
CBHW081545040426
42448CB00015B/3229